I0459399

Scam Destroyer

Your complete pocket guide to spotting scams, stopping fraudsters, and protecting your money and identity in the digital age.

Written by

ERIC LEBOUTHILLIER

AcraSolution | 2025 1st Edition
www.acrasolution.com

Preface

Who this book is for

Scam Destroyer is for **anyone who wants to protect themselves and their loved ones from fraud—online or offline.**

- If you've ever received a suspicious email, text, or phone call and wondered if it was real…
- If you worry about elderly parents being tricked, or kids falling for online traps…
- If you've seen stories of people losing thousands to romance scams, crypto cons, or fake debt collectors and thought, *"That could be me"*…

This book is for you.

It's designed for **everyday people**, not cybersecurity experts. Whether you're a student, a working professional, a retiree, or a busy parent, the lessons inside are simple, clear, and immediately useful.

What to expect from this book

This is not a long, technical manual full of jargon. *Scam Destroyer* is a **pocket-sized, no-filler handbook** you can pick up, flip through, and apply instantly. Inside, you'll find:

- **The Most Common Scams Today** — from old-school phone cons to modern phishing emails, fake online shops, and AI-powered deepfake frauds.
- **Red Flag Checklists** — simple bullet-point lists that make spotting scams quick and easy.
- **Real-World Examples** — screenshots, stories, and breakdowns that show you exactly how scams trick people.
- **Fast Defense Strategies** — clear, practical steps you can take the moment a scam targets you.

- **Lifetime Protection Habits** — simple rules that keep you safe, no matter how scams evolve in the future.

By the end of this book, you'll be able to **spot scams instantly, shut down fraudsters with confidence, and protect your money, time, and peace of mind.**

Copyright © 2025
All Rights Reserved

LEGAL DISCLAIMER

This publication is intended solely for informational and educational purposes. It does not constitute legal, financial, medical, or professional advice. The content is not a substitute for consultation with qualified experts or licensed professionals in the relevant fields.

Portions of this work have been created or assisted by artificial intelligence (AI) tools. While every reasonable effort has been made to review, fact-check, and edit the content for clarity and accuracy, AI-generated information may occasionally contain errors, omissions, or generalized statements. The author and publisher do not guarantee the accuracy, completeness, or reliability of the information provided.

Readers are strongly encouraged to seek independent advice tailored to their personal circumstances from qualified legal, financial, healthcare, or compliance professionals before making decisions or taking action based on this content.

References to specific products, services, companies, websites, or technologies do not imply endorsement or affiliation unless explicitly stated. All trademarks and brand names mentioned remain the property of their respective owners.

The author and publisher disclaim any liability, loss, or risk incurred directly or indirectly from the use or misuse of this publication. This includes, but is not limited to, damages of any kind — including incidental, special, or consequential — arising out of the reliance on the material presented.

All references to laws, regulations, security standards, or industry guidelines are intended for general awareness only and may not reflect the most current legal developments. This publication is not intended to create, and receipt does not constitute, a client relationship with the author, publisher, or any affiliated entity.

By reading, accessing, or applying the content in this publication, you agree to do so at your own risk. If you do not accept these terms, you are advised to discontinue use of this material immediately.

Table of Contents

CHAPTER 1

Phone & Street Scams

Everyday Scams — How Ordinary Tricks Steal Trust

Not all scams unfold in dark corners of the internet. Many come through the most familiar channels: a phone call, a knock at the door, or a request to donate to charity. These cons succeed precisely because they feel routine, blending into the rhythms of daily life. To grow more resilient, we need to recognize their forms, understand why they work, and adopt simple habits that neutralize their power.

Phone Fraud and Robocalls — Authority Over the Line

The phone is still a scammer's most powerful tool. Robocalls flood millions of numbers daily, often using "spoofed" caller IDs to mimic local numbers or trusted institutions. You might see a call labeled *"IRS," "Bank Security,"* or even your own number, designed to bypass your skepticism.

The script is always urgent: *"Your account will be frozen unless you verify now,"* or *"There is a warrant for your arrest unless you pay immediately."* These calls succeed because they combine two triggers—authority and fear. We've been conditioned to respect official voices, and scammers exploit that reflex. But in reality, government agencies, banks, and utilities never demand immediate payment or sensitive details over the phone.

Fake Charities — Exploiting Empathy

Another common scam weaponizes compassion. After disasters, during holidays, or in times of crisis, fake charities appear asking for donations. The plea might come as a text message, an email, or even a friendly voice at your door. The emotional pull is powerful—when people are suffering, we want to act fast to help.

But scammers use urgency to block verification. They may name-drop disasters or recognizable organizations, yet redirect donations to personal accounts or shell companies. After Hurricane Katrina and other major tragedies, billions of dollars were stolen this way. Real generosity was turned into profit for criminals.

Door-to-Door Cons — Deception on the Threshold

The doorstep has long been a stage for scams. Someone arrives in a uniform or with a clipboard, posing as a utility worker, contractor, or salesperson. They may claim your roof needs immediate repair, your electricity will be cut off unless you pay cash, or they're offering a special deal "today only."

Face-to-face interaction makes these scams persuasive. A smile, a badge (even counterfeit), or confident body language lowers our defenses. But urgency and pressure are the giveaway. Genuine services will always allow you to check credentials, call the company directly, or schedule work without immediate payment.

Why These Cons Work

Scams like these succeed not because people are gullible, but because they exploit universal instincts:

- **Trust in authority.** We are taught to respect officials and institutions.
- **Impulse to help.** Empathy is natural, but con artists weaponize it.

- **Social pressure.** Face-to-face encounters make saying "no" feel uncomfortable.

When these instincts are triggered with urgency, we act first and question later. That's exactly what scammers count on.

The Takeaway

Fraud thrives in the ordinary—our phones, our neighborhoods, our willingness to care. But awareness creates a shield. The more familiar we are with these patterns, the quicker we can pause, verify, and refuse manipulation. Growth here is about sharpening instincts: not losing compassion or trust, but balancing them with clarity and caution. By doing so, we protect not just our money, but our confidence in navigating the world.

Red Flags of a Scam — The Patterns You Can't Ignore

Scammers rely on speed and emotion to catch people off guard. They know that if you stop to think, you'll see through the act. That's why their tactics often share the same telltale signs—patterns that repeat across phone fraud, fake charities, door-to-door schemes, and countless other cons. Recognizing these red flags turns confusion into clarity and transforms you from a target into a defender of your own boundaries.

Threats and Intimidation — Fear as a Weapon

One of the strongest warning signs is the use of threats. A caller might say, *"The police are on their way if you don't pay now,"* or *"Your account will be permanently locked unless you act immediately."* Door-to-door con artists may warn that your house is unsafe, claiming urgent repairs are needed to avoid disaster.

These statements are designed to bypass reason and trigger panic. Fear narrows our focus, making us more likely to obey without questioning. But in reality, no legitimate government agency or business communicates by threatening punishment over the phone or at your door. True professionals inform, they do not intimidate.

Cash-Only Demands — Untraceable Transactions

Another common signal is the demand for cash-only payments, wire transfers, or gift cards. These methods are impossible to reverse once money changes hands. A scammer might insist, *"We can't accept checks or credit cards—cash only,"* or ask you to read off numbers from prepaid gift cards.

Legitimate organizations never operate this way. Real charities, service providers, and government institutions offer secure, traceable payment options. The moment someone insists on untraceable funds, assume the worst.

No Way to Verify — Cutting Off Alternatives

The third major red flag is the refusal to let you independently confirm their story. Scammers discourage you from calling back, checking online, or consulting someone else. They'll say, *"You can only resolve this right now, through me,"* or, *"Don't hang up— you'll lose your chance."*

This is intentional. Verification is the enemy of deception. If you take even a few minutes to check an official website, call a trusted number, or ask a friend, the scam collapses. That's why scammers push isolation and urgency: they don't want you to step outside their script.

The Takeaway

Threats, cash-only demands, and blocked verification are not minor details—they are universal fingerprints of fraud. By learning to spot them, you gain a simple but powerful filter: if any of these appear, stop immediately. Growth here means trusting your ability to slow down and question what feels off. Scammers depend on blind reaction; awareness is what takes their power away.

Defenses Against Scams — Practical Moves That Work

Scammers succeed when they keep people reacting instead of thinking. The key to protection is not elaborate technology or memorizing every scam variation—it's developing simple, repeatable habits that interrupt manipulation. By adopting just a few defensive moves, anyone can create a strong barrier against fraud.

Hang Up — Ending the Script

The simplest defense is also the hardest to practice: hang up. Scammers thrive on engagement. Every extra second you stay on the line increases their chance of hooking you emotionally. They know how to escalate pressure, layer in authority, and exploit hesitation.

If something feels off, end the call immediately—without explanation, apology, or debate. Legitimate institutions will never penalize you for disconnecting and calling back through official numbers. Hanging up reclaims your time, your attention, and your control.

Verify Independently — Trust, But Check

Scams often crumble under the light of verification. If someone claims to be from your bank, call the bank directly using the number on your card or their official website. If a charity reaches out, look them up through trusted databases before giving. If a door-to-door worker appears, check their company online and confirm credentials before allowing access.

Verification works because it shifts you out of the scammer's controlled environment. They depend on you staying inside their script. By checking from a trusted source, you step outside their manipulation and see the truth.

Never Pay on the Spot — Buy Time, Gain Clarity

Immediate payment is the scammer's goal. Whether it's cash, wire transfers, or gift cards, they want your money before you have time to think. A firm personal rule—*never pay on the spot*—removes their leverage entirely.

Legitimate organizations allow time. A real contractor provides written estimates. A genuine charity welcomes scheduled donations. Even true emergencies do not require instant transactions with strangers. By refusing to pay immediately, you give yourself the space to assess, confirm, and decide rationally.

The Takeaway

Defending against scams doesn't require paranoia—it requires practice. Hang up when pressured, verify before acting, and never hand over money on the spot. These three habits act like armor, transforming fear into confidence. Growth means not just avoiding loss, but also strengthening your ability to respond with calm clarity when others attempt to manipulate you. In doing so, you protect both your resources and your peace of mind.

CHAPTER 2

Romance & Trust Scams

Digital Deception — The Hidden Dangers of Online Relationships

The internet has transformed how people connect. Friendships, romances, and communities can form across continents in a matter of hours. But with this new intimacy comes new risks. Scammers exploit the very qualities that make online relationships appealing— trust, vulnerability, and hope. Whether it's online dating fraud, catfishing, or fake friendships, these cons strike at one of the deepest human needs: belonging.

Online Dating Fraud — Romance with a Price Tag

Romance scams are among the costliest types of fraud worldwide. They usually begin with an attractive profile on a dating app or social media site. The scammer builds trust over weeks or months, sending daily messages, sharing fabricated details of their "life," and creating the illusion of a genuine relationship.

The turning point comes when money enters the conversation. A sudden crisis arises: *"I need money for a medical emergency,"* or *"I can't afford the ticket to come see you."* Because the emotional bond feels real, many victims transfer funds—sometimes repeatedly.

The Federal Trade Commission reports that romance scams cost Americans over $1 billion annually. What makes them effective is not the story itself, but the emotional investment people have already made. Once feelings of love or attachment are engaged, rational judgment becomes harder to access.

Catfishing — The Mask of Identity

Catfishing is the use of a false persona to lure others into relationships online. Sometimes it's for money, but often it's for control, attention, or amusement. Fake photos, stolen biographies, and fabricated backstories create a convincing mask.

The danger lies in how convincing these identities can be. A catfish may send dozens of carefully staged photos, invent family members, or use real-time video with altered filters. Victims often describe realizing that the relationship felt "more real than real life" until the truth unraveled.

Psychologically, catfishing exploits the *confirmation bias*: when we want something to be true—like finding the perfect partner—we ignore evidence to the contrary. The fantasy becomes more appealing than reality, making it harder to see red flags.

Fake Friendships — Emotional Investment as Currency

Not every scammer seeks romance. Some build false friendships in gaming communities, social media groups, or support forums. They present themselves as supportive, loyal companions, slowly gaining trust before exploiting it—whether through financial requests, blackmail, or manipulation.

One common pattern is the *"sob story scam."* The fraudster shares increasingly dramatic personal struggles—illness, eviction, family crises—until the friend feels morally obligated to help. These situations feel less like cons and more like loyalty tests, which is why victims often ignore their own doubts.

The Takeaway

Digital connections can be powerful and life-changing, but they also provide fertile ground for deception. Growth in this space means balancing openness with discernment. If a new relationship quickly involves secrecy, financial requests, or inconsistencies in their story, it's worth pausing. Genuine connections can withstand questions and verification; fraudulent ones cannot. By learning to trust slowly, verify carefully, and guard against emotional shortcuts, you protect not only your money but also the deeper resource at stake—your trust in human connection.

Red Flags in Online Relationships — When Connection Turns into Control

Most online relationships start with excitement: the thrill of meeting someone new, the possibility of love or deep friendship. But not all digital connections are genuine. Scammers and manipulators know how to mimic affection while hiding behind carefully built personas. The best defense is knowing the red flags—especially when someone avoids accountability or tries to turn emotional connection into financial gain.

Avoids Video Calls — Hiding Behind the Screen

One of the strongest warning signs in online dating or digital friendships is consistent avoidance of live interaction. A scammer might agree to a video chat but cancel at the last minute, citing poor internet, broken cameras, or personal emergencies. They might rely heavily on text and photos—often stolen from real people—while resisting any form of real-time validation.

This pattern is not about shyness. It's about control. Video calls make it much harder to sustain a fake identity. Someone invested in building trust with you will eventually welcome face-to-face interaction, even virtually. Someone avoiding it repeatedly is protecting a deception.

Requests for Money — Emotional Leverage in Disguise

The clearest red flag in online scams is when money enters the relationship. It often begins with small requests, framed as emergencies or tests of loyalty: *"My paycheck is late and I need groceries,"* or *"I just need help with travel so I can finally meet you."* Over time, the asks escalate into medical bills, debt crises, or business "opportunities."

Psychologically, this tactic exploits the *consistency principle*: once you've given once, you're more likely to give again to stay aligned with your past behavior. The scammer builds emotional stakes— suggesting that refusal to send money equals refusal to care. In healthy relationships, financial support is never demanded as proof of love or friendship.

The Takeaway

When someone consistently avoids video calls or introduces money into an online relationship, caution is not paranoia—it's wisdom. These behaviors are not quirks or misunderstandings; they are predictable red flags of manipulation. Growth here means protecting your time, your finances, and your emotional energy. By trusting actions over words, and by setting firm boundaries, you make space for real connections while filtering out those built on deceit.

Defenses in Digital Relationships — How to Protect Your Heart and Wallet

Online connections can be meaningful, but they also carry hidden risks. Scammers know how to fabricate trust with stolen photos, polished scripts, and carefully staged emotions. Fortunately, you don't need advanced tools or endless suspicion to protect yourself. A few clear defenses can expose deception early and safeguard both your finances and your peace of mind.

Reverse Image Search — Revealing the Mask

One of the most effective tools against online deception is the reverse image search. Scammers often steal profile pictures from real people—models, social media users, or even stock photography. By uploading these photos into a search engine, you can see where else they appear online.

If the same image shows up under multiple names, on modeling sites, or in unrelated contexts, that's a strong indicator of fraud. Even a single mismatch—like a person claiming to be a doctor in Chicago, but the photo linking to an actor in Spain—unravels the story.

Using this tool doesn't mean you're paranoid; it means you're verifying. Genuine people have no issue with their identity being consistent across platforms. Only those hiding behind stolen images need to fear scrutiny.

Never Send Money — Protecting Your Boundaries

The simplest and most powerful defense against online scams is an unbreakable rule: never send money to someone you haven't met in person and verified thoroughly. Scammers thrive on creating scenarios that feel urgent or emotionally binding: a sudden illness, travel costs to finally "meet," or family emergencies.

But real relationships do not begin with financial tests. If someone ties affection, loyalty, or commitment to your willingness to transfer money, it's not love or friendship—it's exploitation. Setting this boundary not only protects your bank account but also sends a clear signal: you value trust and transparency over emotional manipulation.

The Takeaway

Scams in digital spaces often succeed because they blur emotions with urgency. But with two simple defenses—reverse image searching suspicious profiles and refusing to send money under any circumstances—you strip these schemes of their power. Growth means staying open to genuine connection while protecting your dignity and resources. By demanding proof and drawing firm boundaries, you ensure that the relationships you invest in are built on truth, not deception.

CHAPTER 3

Email & Text (Phishing/Smishing)

Digital Impersonation — How Everyday Messages Turn into Traps

Inboxes and text threads have become prime hunting grounds for scammers. Instead of complex hacks, many frauds rely on simple messages designed to look routine: a bank alert, a delivery update, or a password reset. These scams are effective because they mimic the rhythm of real life. We're used to quick notifications and fast responses, so we rarely stop to question their authenticity.

Fake Bank Alerts — Fear in Your Pocket

A common tactic is the fraudulent bank alert. A text or email might read: *"Suspicious activity detected. Click here to secure your account."* The urgency is deliberate. By suggesting your money is at risk, scammers push you to act without thinking.

The link usually leads to a convincing fake website where victims enter their login details—handing over the keys to their real accounts. Some even ask for two-factor authentication codes in real time, bypassing security measures.

The truth: banks never require you to click a link in a message to confirm security. They direct you to log in through official apps or websites. If you're being rushed to act through a text, assume it's a scam.

Delivery Texts — The Package That Doesn't Exist

Another rising scam involves fake delivery notifications. A message might claim, *"Your package is waiting. Pay customs fee here,"* or *"Delivery attempt failed. Reschedule now."* With online shopping so common, these alerts feel plausible.

But the links lead to malware downloads or payment portals controlled by scammers. The trick works because of timing—during holiday seasons or after placing real orders, people expect delivery messages. Scammers exploit that normal expectation to slip in unnoticed.

Password Reset Scams — Identity on the Line

Password reset scams exploit trust in technology. An email may say, *"Your account password has been reset. If this wasn't you, click here."* The message creates panic—who wouldn't worry about being hacked?

But the link directs you to a fake login page. By entering your credentials, you hand them directly to criminals. The psychological hook here is urgency combined with fear of losing control. Victims often click before considering whether they requested a reset in the first place.

The Takeaway

Scams thrive by impersonating the ordinary. Bank alerts, delivery updates, and password resets are all familiar messages, which is why they're so effective when faked. Growth in the digital age means slowing down the instinct to click immediately. Real institutions give you time and secure ways to verify. If a message demands instant action, it's almost always a trap. By pausing, checking independently, and refusing to engage through suspicious links, you protect not just your money but also your digital identity.

Red Flags in Digital Messages — How to Read Between the Lines

Fraudulent texts and emails are designed to look ordinary at first glance. But closer inspection usually reveals cracks in the disguise. Scammers rely on speed—your quick click—so they don't expect you to pause and notice the details. By training yourself to look for three common signs, you can catch many scams before they catch you: misspellings, urgency, and suspicious links.

Misspellings and Awkward Language — The Hidden Tell

Many scam messages contain spelling errors, grammatical mistakes, or awkward phrasing. You might see a bank message that says, *"Your acccount is been locked,"* or a delivery notice with phrases like *"Click hear for reschedual."*

These aren't always accidents. Some fraudsters intentionally include mistakes to filter out cautious readers. If you overlook obvious errors, they assume you're more likely to fall for the rest of the scheme. Either way, poor language is a reliable sign that the message didn't come from a professional institution.

Urgency — Act Now or Lose Everything

Almost every scam includes a time limit: *"Respond within 24 hours," "Your account will be closed today," "Final notice."* Urgency is a psychological shortcut. It pressures you to act before you reflect.

Legitimate companies rarely impose immediate deadlines through text or email, especially when money or personal information is involved. If a message insists you must act right now, treat it as suspicious until verified.

Weird Links — The Trap Behind the Click

Suspicious links are the core of most phishing scams. At first glance, they might look legitimate: *"pay-pal.com.verify123.net"* or *"amaz0n-support.co."* But if you look closely, the domain is slightly altered.

Clicking these links usually leads to fake login pages or malware downloads. The safest practice is never to click directly. Instead, navigate to the company's official website by typing the address yourself or using their official app. If the request is real, you'll find it there.

The Takeaway

Scams reveal themselves in patterns: sloppy spelling, pressure to act fast, and links that don't quite match. Once you know to look for these signs, your inbox becomes less of a minefield and more of a map. Growth means not just avoiding the traps, but also building confidence in your ability to read critically. By spotting red flags early, you stay one step ahead of the manipulation.

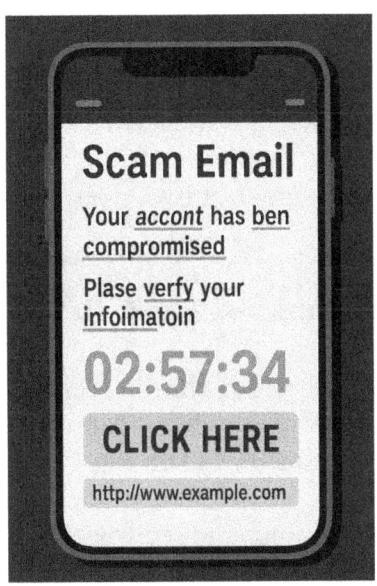

Defenses Against Digital Scams — Staying One Step Ahead

Fraudulent emails and texts succeed when we respond automatically. A quick click or hasty login is all it takes to hand over valuable information. The strongest defense is not paranoia but discipline—developing habits that keep you in control. Two simple practices can block most digital scams before they even begin: verifying through official channels and refusing to click blind links.

Verify Through Official Apps and Websites

When a message claims to be from your bank, delivery service, or email provider, never act through the message itself. Instead, go directly to the source. Use your bank's mobile app, type the official website address into your browser, or call customer service through the number printed on the back of your card.

This habit removes the scammer's leverage. Their fake alerts only work if you stay inside the environment they control—the email, the text, or the link they provide. The moment you step outside and check through official channels, the fraud collapses.

For example, if you receive a "failed delivery" notice, check your order history on the store's official website. If it's real, the notification will be there too. If it isn't, you've saved yourself from a costly mistake.

Never Click Blind Links — Pause Before You Tap

Suspicious links are the heart of phishing scams. They redirect you to fake login pages, install malware, or capture sensitive data. The easiest defense? Never click links you can't fully verify.

Hover over links on a computer to see where they actually lead. On a phone, press and hold to preview the URL. If it looks strange—extra numbers, misspellings, or odd domains—don't touch it. And even if it looks legitimate, the safest move is to type the official address yourself or use the trusted app.

This small pause is powerful. Scammers count on you reacting instantly to urgency. By breaking that reflex, you take back control.

The Takeaway

Defending against digital scams doesn't require advanced tech skills—just consistent habits. Verify messages through official apps and websites, and never click blind links, no matter how convincing they appear. Growth in the digital world means moving from reaction to reflection: slowing down, double-checking, and trusting your caution. With these simple defenses, you build digital resilience that protects not only your accounts but also your peace of mind.

CHAPTER 4

Social Media & Online Scams

The Illusion of Online Opportunity — Giveaways, Hacks, and Influencer Cons

The digital world thrives on attention. Social media platforms are filled with giveaways, influencer promotions, and shared links that promise something valuable. But where attention flows, manipulation follows. Scammers exploit trust in familiar names— friends, celebrities, or influencers—to create schemes that look like opportunities but end as traps.

Fake Giveaways — The Prize That Costs You

Giveaway scams often appear in the form of social media posts or messages: *"Congratulations! You've won—just click this link to claim your prize."* Sometimes the scam mimics real promotions by reputable brands, using stolen logos and professional-looking graphics.

The catch? To "claim" the reward, victims are asked for shipping fees, taxes, or personal information such as credit card details. Some links even install malware. The irony is that instead of receiving a prize, the victim ends up paying or exposing sensitive data.

Real giveaways never require payment to collect a prize. If a contest feels rushed, unclear, or too good to be true, it usually is.

Hacked Accounts — Trust Turned Against You

Another common tactic is account takeovers. A hacked social media account begins sending messages to friends: *"Check out this investment opportunity,"* or *"Can you help me out with some money quickly?"* Because the request appears to come from someone you know, it bypasses skepticism.

These scams spread quickly because victims often comply before realizing the account has been compromised. By the time suspicion arises, the scammer has already moved on to new targets.

The lesson: trust the person, but verify the message. If a friend suddenly sends an unusual link or request, confirm through another channel before engaging.

Influencer Cons — Fame as a Shortcut

Scammers also hijack the credibility of influencers. Fake accounts copy popular figures, promising exclusive deals, investment tips, or private access. Sometimes even real influencers are manipulated into promoting fraudulent products, lured by sponsorship offers that turn out to be scams themselves.

The psychology here is simple: authority bias. We assume that if someone with followers endorses something, it must be legitimate. But scammers know this bias and exploit it ruthlessly. Even a verified-looking profile can be fake, and "limited-time offers" are often engineered traps.

The Takeaway

Fake giveaways, hacked accounts, and influencer scams all exploit the same human tendencies—our trust in familiar names and our attraction to easy rewards. Growth in this area means building a healthy skepticism without losing optimism. Verify giveaways through official brand pages, confirm unusual messages with friends, and remember that influence is not the same as credibility. When you pause before acting, you protect yourself not just from losing money, but from losing faith in the connections that make digital life meaningful.

Red Flags in Social Media Scams — Reading the Signals Before It's Too Late

Scammers on social platforms rarely rely on complex tricks. Instead, they lean on patterns that trigger excitement or urgency, hoping you'll click before thinking. Two of the most common signals—"too-good-to-be-true" offers and urgent direct messages—show up again and again across fake giveaways, hacked accounts, and influencer cons. Learning to spot them early is one of the strongest defenses you can build.

Too-Good-to-Be-True Offers — The Bait of Easy Rewards

If a message promises instant wealth, exclusive deals, or guaranteed prizes, pause. Real opportunities come with effort, competition, or clear conditions. Scams, by contrast, exaggerate rewards and minimize risk: *"Win $5,000 instantly just by sharing this post,"* or *"Double your money in 24 hours."*

Psychologists call this *reward salience*: when a potential gain feels unusually large or easy, it hijacks our attention and judgment. But the imbalance is the giveaway. If the prize looks far greater than the effort required, it's almost certainly a lure.

Urgent DMs — Pressure Behind the Curtain

Scammers also exploit urgency through direct messages. You might receive a sudden DM from a "friend" or influencer saying, *"You must act now—this offer ends tonight,"* or *"I need your help urgently, please send money."* These messages work because they bypass public scrutiny; nobody else sees the pressure, and you feel singled out.

Urgency narrows focus and creates a false deadline. Real businesses and genuine friends respect your time and allow for verification.

When a private message insists you act before thinking, it's a red flag that someone is trying to trap you.

The Takeaway

Scams on social media aren't random—they're predictable. Too-good-to-be-true offers and urgent private messages are signals that should always spark caution. Growth in the digital age means resisting the reflex to click or respond immediately. By stepping back, checking sources, and remembering that real opportunities withstand scrutiny, you protect not just your wallet but also your trust in the communities where you connect.

Defenses on Social Media — How to Stay Safe While Staying Connected

Social platforms are powerful spaces for connection, but they are also fertile ground for scams. The best protection isn't withdrawing completely—it's practicing habits that keep you safe while still allowing you to engage fully. Two defenses stand out above the rest: always verifying before acting and refusing to share personal information with untrusted sources.

Verify Before You Trust

Scammers depend on speed. They want you to click, respond, or send money before you have time to think. Verification disrupts that cycle. If a brand claims you've won a giveaway, check their official account or website. If a friend messages you with an unusual request, call or text them directly to confirm. If an influencer promotes an "exclusive" deal, cross-check their actual verified page or other reliable sources.

Verification puts you back in control. It takes minutes, but it's enough to reveal whether an opportunity is genuine or a trap. Real offers and real friends will hold up under scrutiny—only scams fall apart when questioned.

Don't Share Personal Information

Scams often succeed not because of what they promise, but because of what they extract. Fraudsters may ask for phone numbers, email addresses, bank details, or even copies of IDs under the guise of "claiming a prize" or "confirming identity." Once shared, this data can be sold, used to open accounts, or leveraged in future attacks.

The simplest rule: never give personal information through social media DMs, comments, or links, no matter how official they look. Legitimate companies use secure websites and verified processes for sensitive details—not casual messages. Protecting your information is protecting your identity.

The Takeaway

Scammers thrive on blind trust, but they can't survive healthy skepticism. By making verification your first step and guarding your personal details as tightly as your bank card, you build a shield against digital deception. Growth in this space means staying open to connection while refusing to be careless with trust. With these habits, you can enjoy the benefits of social media without becoming prey to its hidden risks.

CHAPTER 5

Online Shopping & Marketplaces

Marketplace Manipulation — How Scammers Exploit Buying and Selling

Online marketplaces and resale platforms have made buying and selling more convenient than ever. But with convenience comes exposure to new types of fraud. Fake listings, counterfeit goods, and auction scams all thrive on the trust we place in digital transactions. By understanding how these schemes work, we can shop and sell with confidence instead of fear.

Fake Listings — Selling What Doesn't Exist

One of the most common scams is the fake listing. A seller advertises a popular item—concert tickets, gaming consoles, high-end electronics—at an irresistible price. The urgency is high: *"Only one left, act fast!"* Once payment is made, the seller disappears. The product never existed.

These scams exploit the scarcity effect. When an item feels rare or in high demand, we're more willing to overlook red flags and rush into the purchase. Scammers know this and craft offers designed to feel like once-in-a-lifetime deals.

Counterfeit Goods — Paying Premium for Fakes

Counterfeit scams don't leave you empty-handed, but the item you receive isn't what you paid for. From luxury handbags to electronics, counterfeiters produce convincing copies, complete with fake logos, packaging, and certificates.

The psychology here is prestige bias: people value branded goods as status symbols, and scammers exploit that desire by offering them at "discounted" prices. Buyers convince themselves they've found a bargain, only to discover they've paid premium prices for knockoffs worth a fraction of the cost.

Auction Scams — Manipulating the Bid

Auction platforms create excitement by turning shopping into competition. But some auctions are rigged. Fraudsters use shill bidding—placing fake bids to inflate the price—or create entire auction sites that never deliver goods once the money is transferred.

The thrill of "winning" fuels these scams. Bidding wars trigger emotional investment, making people more likely to pay higher prices than planned and less likely to question legitimacy once they've "won."

The Takeaway

Marketplace scams succeed because they hijack trust, urgency, and the desire for value. Growth here means resisting the impulse to rush and learning to pause before purchasing. Real sellers provide verifiable details, traceable payment methods, and transparency. Fake ones push you to decide quickly, pay upfront, and skip verification. By slowing down and scrutinizing offers, you can enjoy the benefits of online marketplaces without becoming a victim of their traps.

Red Flags in Online Marketplaces — Spotting the Hidden Cons

Shopping online feels effortless—click, pay, receive. But scammers rely on that very convenience to slip in fraudulent offers. Two of the most reliable red flags are offers with unusually deep discounts and sellers who lack credible reviews. Learning to spot these signals helps you separate genuine deals from costly traps.

Deep Discounts — When the Price Doesn't Add Up

If a luxury handbag is listed at 80% off or a brand-new gaming console is half the retail price, it's not luck—it's bait. Scammers use extreme discounts to create urgency, hoping buyers will act before questioning authenticity. This taps into the scarcity effect: when we think we've found a rare bargain, we feel pressured to grab it before someone else does.

While real discounts exist, they rarely appear on high-demand or brand-new items. If a price seems dramatically below market value, it usually means the product doesn't exist or it's a counterfeit. A good rule: if the deal feels unbelievable, believe your instincts—it's a trap.

No Reviews — Silence Speaks Volumes

Another red flag is the absence of seller history or credible reviews. Reputable sellers build trust through consistent ratings, detailed feedback, and verified transactions. Scammers, by contrast, often operate with brand-new accounts, minimal information, or suspiciously vague testimonials.

In marketplaces where reviews can be manipulated, watch for patterns: repeated phrases, overly generic praise, or accounts that have only ever reviewed one seller. A lack of verifiable reputation means you're taking the risk blind—and that's exactly what scammers want.

The Takeaway

Deep discounts and missing reviews are not minor details—they are warning sirens. Scammers rely on buyers ignoring these signals in the excitement of a "deal." Growth means slowing down enough to check: compare prices across platforms, read seller history carefully, and trust caution over impulse. Real value comes from safe, verified purchases—not from bargains that vanish the moment you pay.

Defenses in Online Marketplaces — Buying Without Fear

Digital marketplaces are powerful tools, but they're also crowded with fraud. The good news is that you don't need to avoid them altogether—you just need to shop with structure. The strongest defenses come from choosing secure platforms and insisting on buyer protection for every transaction.

Use Secure Platforms — Safety in Systems

Not all marketplaces are created equal. Established platforms invest heavily in fraud prevention, identity verification, and transaction monitoring. They provide encrypted payments and systems that track sellers' histories, helping you spot bad actors before it's too late.

Scammers often push buyers away from these systems. They may suggest paying "off-platform" via wire transfer, gift cards, or direct bank deposits, claiming it will "save fees" or "speed up delivery." This is a trap. Once money leaves the official channel, it's untraceable and unrecoverable.

The rule is simple: if a seller insists on bypassing the platform's payment system, walk away. A safe seller is never afraid of accountability.

Insist on Buyer Protection — Your Digital Insurance

Buyer protection is like insurance for online shopping. Many secure platforms hold funds in escrow until the buyer confirms receipt, refund payments when items aren't delivered, or mediate disputes when goods are counterfeit. These safeguards exist to level the playing field between anonymous strangers.

Fraudsters hate buyer protection, which is why they avoid platforms that provide it. By sticking with systems that guarantee refunds or dispute resolution, you shift power away from scammers and back into your hands.

The Takeaway

Online marketplaces don't have to feel like a gamble. By choosing secure platforms and making buyer protection a non-negotiable, you reduce risk without sacrificing convenience. Growth here means developing habits of patience and caution: refusing shortcuts, trusting structure, and demanding accountability. In the long run, safety isn't about missing out on deals—it's about ensuring that every deal you make is real.

CHAPTER 6

Investment & Money Scams

The Mirage of Wealth — Ponzi Schemes, Get-Rich-Quick Traps, and Modern Tech Scams

The promise of fast money has always been irresistible. From the earliest gold rushes to the latest digital currencies, people are drawn to shortcuts that appear to skip the slow grind of work and investment. Scammers know this, and they've refined ways to package illusions of wealth so convincingly that even seasoned professionals sometimes fall for them. Ponzi schemes, "get rich quick" traps, and modern scams around crypto, NFTs, and AI are all variations of the same trick: exploiting hope, greed, and trust in new opportunities.

Ponzi Schemes — The Oldest Financial Trick

Named after Charles Ponzi, who in the 1920s promised investors huge returns through a postage stamp arbitrage scam, Ponzi schemes remain one of the most enduring forms of fraud. The model is simple: early investors are paid with money from newer investors, creating the illusion of steady profits. As long as fresh money flows in, the scheme looks legitimate.

What makes Ponzi schemes effective is their believability. They don't promise overnight riches, but rather consistent, slightly above-average returns. This "plausible success" lowers suspicion. Bernie Madoff, who orchestrated the largest Ponzi scheme in history, promised returns of around 10–12% annually—just enough to seem reasonable, but steady enough to hook even wealthy, experienced clients.

The collapse is inevitable. When new investments dry up or too many people request withdrawals, the scheme unravels. By then, billions may be lost, and trust destroyed. The lesson: if returns are steady regardless of market conditions, and if transparency about how profits are made is absent, caution is essential.

Get-Rich-Quick Traps — The Psychology of the Shortcut

Beyond Ponzi structures, scammers prey on the universal desire for shortcuts. Ads or influencers claim, *"Turn $500 into $5,000 in a week,"* or *"Quit your job in 30 days with this secret system."* These schemes often involve multi-level marketing structures, fake coaching programs, or fabricated investment platforms.

Psychologically, these appeals exploit the *scarcity heuristic* ("limited time only"), the *fear of missing out (FOMO)*, and the *illusion of control*—the idea that success is guaranteed if you just follow simple steps. The danger isn't only financial. Many victims invest not only money but time, energy, and self-belief into these programs. When they collapse, the damage to confidence can be deeper than the financial loss.

Crypto, NFTs, and AI Fraud — Old Tricks in New Clothing

In recent years, scammers have moved into cutting-edge spaces: cryptocurrencies, non-fungible tokens (NFTs), and artificial intelligence startups. The pitch is always the same: *"This is the future—get in early before it's too late."*

- **Crypto scams** often involve fake exchanges, pump-and-dump coins, or phishing schemes that steal digital wallets. Because crypto is complex and unregulated in many places, scammers thrive on confusion.
- **NFT scams** promise unique digital assets or investment-grade collectibles. Victims may buy images with no real ownership rights or invest in projects that disappear overnight.
- **AI fraud** is the newest wave, with startups claiming revolutionary tools or algorithms, often backed by fabricated demos or stolen research. Investors, eager not to miss the "next big thing," pour in money without due diligence.

Each of these scams exploits the halo effect of technology. When something is new and technical, people assume it must also be valuable. Combine that with social proof—celebrities or influencers hyping projects—and the illusion becomes even harder to resist.

Why We Fall for the Mirage

Across all these frauds, the psychological levers are consistent:

- **Greed and hope.** The desire for financial freedom makes us overlook risk.
- **Social proof.** If others are investing—friends, celebrities, or early adopters—we fear being left behind.
- **Complexity.** When we don't fully understand something, we often defer to those who seem confident. Scammers count on this gap in knowledge.

Defenses Against the Illusion

Protecting yourself doesn't mean avoiding all new opportunities—it means grounding them in reality. A few core defenses apply across Ponzi schemes, get-rich-quick traps, and modern tech fraud:

1. **Check the source.** Verify whether the company or project is registered, licensed, or audited. Scammers avoid scrutiny.
2. **Question steady or extreme returns.** Real investments fluctuate. Guaranteed profit is almost always a lie.
3. **Avoid urgency.** If someone says *"invest now or miss out forever,"* that pressure is itself a red flag.
4. **Understand before you invest.** If you can't explain how the business makes money in simple terms, you shouldn't trust it with yours.
5. **Trust transparency over hype.** A legitimate opportunity welcomes questions and provides verifiable proof. Fraudulent ones resist scrutiny.

The Takeaway

Ponzi schemes, get-rich-quick traps, and modern tech scams are all mirrors of the same illusion: wealth without effort, guaranteed returns, access to secrets others don't know. Growth in this area means rewiring how we respond to opportunity. Instead of chasing shortcuts, we learn to prize transparency, patience, and critical thinking. Scammers can only succeed when hope runs faster than caution. By slowing down, asking questions, and demanding proof, you not only protect your money—you strengthen your ability to pursue real growth built on truth, not mirages.

Red Flags of Wealth Scams — The Signals Behind the Hype

Fraudulent investment schemes often sound sophisticated, but beneath the complexity lie simple patterns. No matter whether it's a Ponzi scheme, a "get rich quick" program, or the latest crypto or AI project, the same red flags reappear: guaranteed returns, secrecy, and urgency. Recognizing these signals can mean the difference between protecting your resources and falling for a polished illusion.

Guaranteed Returns — The Lie of Certainty

One of the clearest signs of fraud is the promise of guaranteed profits. You'll hear claims like *"10% every month, no risk,"* or *"Double your investment in 90 days."* These statements are effective because they play to our craving for stability in a world of financial uncertainty.

But in reality, all legitimate investments fluctuate. Even the safest bonds carry risks. When someone eliminates risk entirely, they're selling fantasy, not finance. Ponzi schemes in particular thrive on this promise of consistency—paying steady returns until the structure inevitably collapses.

Secrecy — "Trust Me, Don't Ask"

Another universal red flag is secrecy. Scammers often claim they have a "proprietary method," "exclusive strategy," or "inside information" that can't be explained. They discourage questions, using authority or complexity to silence doubt.

Psychologically, this taps into the *authority bias*—the belief that someone with confidence or credentials must know better. Victims convince themselves, *"If others trust them, I should too."* But true opportunity welcomes scrutiny. If transparency is missing, so is legitimacy.

Urgency — Pressure as a Weapon

The third red flag is urgency. Fraudsters insist you act fast: *"Spots are limited," "Offer ends tonight," "Don't miss this once-in-a-lifetime chance."* This tactic hijacks rational thinking by triggering FOMO—the fear of missing out.

Urgency is rarely a feature of real investments. If an opportunity can't survive a few days of reflection or verification, it wasn't worth pursuing in the first place. Pressure is not a sign of value—it's a sign of manipulation.

The Takeaway

Guaranteed returns, secrecy, and urgency are not details—they are the fingerprints of fraud. They show up whether the scam involves stamps in the 1920s, cryptocurrency in the 2020s, or whatever trend comes next. Growth means refusing to let excitement outrun caution. When you encounter these signals, pause. Ask questions. Verify independently. The right opportunities will withstand your scrutiny; the wrong ones will crumble under it.

Defenses Against Wealth Scams — Grounding Ambition in Reality

Scams built around money and opportunity work because they appeal to something universal: the dream of financial freedom. Ponzi schemes, "get rich quick" programs, and the newest waves of crypto, NFT, and AI fraud all offer shortcuts that seem irresistible. The key to protecting yourself isn't shutting down ambition—it's learning to ground it in reality. Two powerful defenses stand above the rest: thorough research and limiting investments to licensed, verified platforms.

Research — Asking the Questions Scammers Fear

The single greatest enemy of fraud is investigation. Scammers rely on speed, hype, and surface-level trust. They know that if you dig too deep—reading the fine print, checking the history, or asking hard questions—the illusion begins to crack. That's why most fraudulent schemes discourage scrutiny, hiding behind jargon or secrecy.

Research doesn't mean spending weeks analyzing complex whitepapers or memorizing financial reports. It means consistently doing the basics:

- **Verify the team.** Are the people behind the company or project real, traceable, and credible? Can you find consistent records of their careers outside this one venture? Scammers often use stock photos, fake LinkedIn profiles, or stolen identities.
- **Follow the money.** Does the business model make sense? Can you clearly explain how it generates revenue in your own words? If profits sound mysterious or depend solely on new members joining, you're likely looking at a Ponzi or pyramid scheme.
- **Search for history.** Real companies leave a trail: news coverage, regulatory filings, customer reviews, and partnerships. Fake ones usually appear out of nowhere with flashy websites and no external validation.
- **Look for independent reviews.** Don't rely on testimonials posted by the company itself. Check whether third-party sources—trusted journalists, regulators, or professional analysts—have reviewed the opportunity.

The essence of research is slowing down long enough to break the spell of urgency. Scammers can imitate legitimacy, but they cannot survive consistent, independent questioning.

Licensed Platforms Only — Trust Structures, Not Promises

The second major defense is choosing where you place your money. Fraud thrives in unregulated environments, where scammers can create fake exchanges, bogus apps, or shadowy investment "clubs." By contrast, licensed platforms are bound by legal and financial oversight. They may not eliminate risk, but they dramatically reduce the chance of outright fraud.

When considering an investment platform, ask:

- **Is it registered?** In most countries, financial institutions must register with regulators such as the SEC in the United States or the FCA in the United Kingdom. Lack of registration is a glaring warning sign.
- **Does it offer investor protection?** Licensed platforms often provide insurance or refund mechanisms when fraud occurs. Unregulated sites leave you completely exposed.
- **Are the terms transparent?** A legitimate platform will clearly outline fees, risks, and withdrawal procedures. Scammers, by contrast, bury details or avoid them entirely.

Ponzi schemes collapse because they exist outside formal oversight. Get-rich-quick programs thrive because they operate in grey zones, promising opportunities without accountability. By restricting yourself to licensed, verifiable systems, you eliminate the vast majority of fraud attempts before they even reach you.

The Takeaway

Hope and ambition aren't the problem—manipulation is. Scammers prey on the desire for a better life, but they fear skepticism, patience, and structure. By committing to research and using only licensed platforms, you protect yourself without giving up the possibility of real growth.

Growth here means learning to distinguish between opportunity and illusion. A true investment welcomes questions, offers transparency, and operates within established structures. A scam avoids scrutiny, hides behind secrecy, and pressures you to act fast. The more you strengthen these defenses, the less likely you are to lose not just money, but trust in your own financial judgment.

When in doubt, remember this: if an investment can survive your research and stands on the foundation of regulation, it may be worth considering. If it collapses under those tests, you've just saved yourself from becoming someone else's profit.

CHAPTER 7

Job, Loan & Debt Scams

Work, Debt, and False Promises — Scams That Exploit Survival Needs

Not all scams tempt us with wealth or glamour. Some prey on far more basic human needs: the need for work, the need for stability, the need to escape financial pressure. Fraudsters understand that when people are struggling, they may be more willing to take risks, less able to question red flags, and more desperate to believe in solutions. That is why fake job offers, phony "training fees," and fraudulent debt relief programs are among the most damaging scams. They don't just steal money—they exploit hope when it is most fragile.

Fake Job Offers — Employment That Doesn't Exist

Imagine scrolling through your inbox or a job board and seeing an email that says: *"Congratulations! You've been selected for an exciting opportunity. High pay, flexible hours, work from home. No experience needed—apply today!"* At first glance, it feels like luck has finally turned. But this is often the start of a scam.

Fake job offers typically promise easy money and quick hiring, avoiding the rigorous processes of real employers. Victims may be asked to provide sensitive information—Social Security numbers, bank account details for "direct deposit," or copies of IDs. Sometimes, scammers go further, asking for money up front for "starter kits" or special equipment. In reality, there is no job, no employer, and no paycheck waiting.

What makes this scheme powerful is that it mimics the structure of real employment. In uncertain times, people are eager for legitimate remote work or side income. Scammers know this and design offers that feel like they answer exactly those needs.

"Training Fees" — Paying to Work

One variation of the job scam involves training programs. Victims are told they've been "hired," but before starting, they must pay for certification, onboarding materials, or exclusive courses. The fee may seem small at first, but once paid, the scammer disappears—or demands further payments for "advanced training."

This tactic exploits the *sunk cost fallacy*: once someone has invested money, they feel compelled to continue, hoping it will eventually pay off. Real employers, however, never charge employees for training. Companies invest in workers because they benefit from their performance. If payment is required just to begin, it's almost certainly a scam.

Fake Debt Relief — Freedom at a Price

Debt relief scams target a different kind of vulnerability. People under financial strain are told: *"We can erase your debt,"* or *"We'll negotiate with creditors on your behalf."* Victims are often pressured into paying upfront fees or signing contracts that give scammers control of their accounts.

Instead of providing relief, these schemes drain money and sometimes worsen the victim's credit by preventing real payments from being made. What's most cruel is that these scams prey on people already under stress. When you're drowning in bills, the promise of rescue feels irresistible.

Legitimate debt relief does exist, but it comes through licensed credit counselors, nonprofit organizations, or government programs. Real providers are transparent about risks, timelines, and outcomes. Scammers, by contrast, guarantee results that no one can promise— like erasing all debt instantly.

Why These Scams Work

Unlike luxury frauds or speculative investments, these schemes succeed because they target survival instincts. When you need a paycheck, you want to believe in the job. When you're overwhelmed with debt, you want to believe in relief. This emotional pressure narrows perspective and makes red flags easier to overlook.

Psychologically, these scams exploit three powerful forces:

- **Scarcity:** The sense that jobs or financial lifelines are rare, so you can't risk missing one.
- **Authority:** Professional-looking emails, fake company logos, or scripted "interviews" create an illusion of legitimacy.
- **Relief bias:** When people are under stress, they cling to solutions that promise immediate relief, even if they seem too perfect.

Defenses That Work

To protect yourself against these scams, a few practices are essential:

1. **Research the employer or company.** Search their name along with the word "scam." Check whether they have a verified website, professional contact information, and a digital history beyond a flashy ad.
2. **Remember the hiring rule:** real jobs pay you, not the other way around. Any offer that requires you to buy training, kits, or equipment before you start is suspicious.
3. **Verify debt relief providers.** Only work with organizations that are licensed, nonprofit, or recommended by official government resources. Avoid anyone who guarantees total debt forgiveness or demands upfront fees.
4. **Protect your data.** Never share banking details, IDs, or Social Security numbers until you've thoroughly confirmed legitimacy.

The Takeaway

Scammers targeting employment and debt don't just steal money—they exploit dignity and hope. Fake job offers, training fee traps, and fraudulent debt relief programs succeed because they promise survival in moments of desperation. Growth in this area means recognizing that legitimate opportunities always withstand scrutiny. Work should never cost you money, and debt solutions should never be based on secrecy or urgency.

By committing to research, demanding transparency, and trusting caution over desperation, you build resilience not just against fraud, but against the subtle manipulation of your hopes. Real opportunities bring empowerment. Fake ones leave scars. Knowing the difference is one of the most important financial skills you can ever develop.

False Opportunities — When "Work" and "Relief" Cost You Instead

Scams built around jobs and debt relief strike at the very core of survival. Unlike luxury frauds that tempt with wealth or status, these schemes exploit situations where people feel they have no choice but to take a chance. A job offer that seems to solve unemployment, or a debt relief program that promises freedom from crushing bills, can feel like a lifeline. But hidden behind the promise is a cruel trap: instead of receiving help, victims are asked to pay first. Two of the most common red flags in this area are **pay-to-work requirements** and **upfront fees** for services. They flip the natural order of opportunity on its head, asking for sacrifice where there should be support.

Pay-to-Work — A Job That Drains Before It Pays

Legitimate employment is based on a simple principle: the employer invests in the worker, and the worker earns through their labor. Pay-to-work scams invert this, requiring applicants to spend money before starting.

These schemes often appear in the form of:

- **Starter kits.** Victims are told they must buy supplies, uniforms, or tools to qualify.
- **Training programs.** Fraudsters frame mandatory courses as essential preparation, but once fees are paid, the training is worthless—or doesn't exist at all.
- **Equipment purchases.** Scammers claim you'll need to buy a laptop, special software, or licenses to "work from home," often directing you to fake suppliers.

The psychology is effective. The applicant has already envisioned themselves in the role, picturing income and stability. By this stage, resistance feels like throwing away a chance. But the truth is that no legitimate employer demands new hires to pay before earning. Companies cover training costs because they benefit from employee performance. If the payment flows in the opposite direction, it's not a job—it's a purchase disguised as one.

Upfront Fees — Debt Relief That Deepens the Burden

Debt relief scams mirror the same tactic, but they target financial desperation instead of unemployment. Victims are told: *"We can erase your debt,"* or *"We'll negotiate with creditors on your behalf."* But before anything happens, they must pay upfront fees—sometimes hundreds or thousands of dollars.

The fraud works because it dangles hope of immediate relief. For someone facing mounting bills or collection calls, a lump payment can feel like the only way out. But what happens next is predictable:

- The scammer disappears after receiving the fee.
- The company delays until frustration grows, then asks for more money.
- Victims are instructed to stop paying creditors while "negotiations" take place—ruining their credit and making debt worse.

Legitimate credit counseling agencies or licensed debt relief providers are transparent about fees, timelines, and outcomes. They cannot promise to erase all debt instantly. And they never demand large payments upfront before any service begins.

Why People Fall for These Traps

Both pay-to-work and upfront fee scams exploit the psychology of urgency. When someone is jobless or drowning in debt, hesitation feels dangerous. The thought of losing an opportunity can seem worse than risking money.

Scammers craft their pitch carefully to exploit this:

- **Scarcity:** "This is a limited-time position, act now."
- **Authority:** Professional-looking emails, contracts, or websites create a false sense of credibility.
- **Emotional leverage:** They frame payment as an "investment in your future," appealing to optimism and responsibility.

The cruel genius of these scams is that they don't target greed—they target survival. Victims often feel embarrassed afterward, but their choice wasn't foolish; it was human. Scammers simply knew how to weaponize hope.

Defenses That Protect

Protection begins with remembering one core rule: real opportunities do not require you to pay first. Work pays you, not the other way around. Debt relief should remove burdens, not create new ones.

From this foundation, a few practical defenses can make a critical difference:

1. **Research the offer.** Search the company name along with "scam" or "complaints." Fraudulent operations often leave a digital trail of warnings from past victims.
2. **Check credentials.** For debt relief, verify licensing through government or consumer protection agencies. Real providers are registered and regulated.
3. **Refuse upfront fees.** Whether it's for training, equipment, or "processing," reject any offer that requires payment before results.
4. **Protect personal data.** Many scams use fake job offers as a cover to steal identities. Never send Social Security numbers, banking details, or ID copies until the employer is verified.
5. **Pause under pressure.** If an offer insists you decide immediately, that pressure itself is a red flag. Genuine opportunities can wait for questions and confirmation.

The Takeaway

Scams based on fake jobs and fraudulent debt relief do more than steal money—they exploit dignity, need, and hope. They prey on people when they are most vulnerable, flipping opportunity into betrayal. But awareness transforms vulnerability into resilience. Recognizing red flags like pay-to-work schemes and upfront fees gives you a shield against manipulation.

Growth here means refusing to let desperation override judgment. It means slowing down even when the pressure feels urgent, asking hard questions even when the promise feels comforting, and walking away from offers that demand sacrifice before trust has been earned. Real jobs provide income. Real debt relief provides structure and support. Anything else is an illusion, designed to drain those already under strain. By holding to this truth, you protect not only your finances, but also your confidence in navigating hardship with clarity instead of fear.

Defenses Against Job and Debt Scams — Finding Truth in Official Sources

Scams built around fake job offers, bogus training fees, and fraudulent debt relief programs exploit vulnerability. They thrive in moments when people need stability most—when unemployment feels crushing or when bills pile so high that relief seems impossible. Fraudsters know that in these situations, victims often don't stop to question an opportunity. That's why the most effective defenses are not complex—they are about grounding yourself in verified, trustworthy sources before acting. Two of the most powerful safeguards are **using official job boards** and **checking government sites for debt relief programs.**

Why Official Sources Matter

Scammers design their offers to look polished. Fake websites mimic corporate branding. Fraudulent emails carry convincing logos. Social media ads present flashy opportunities that appear legitimate at first glance. If we rely only on surface impressions, it is easy to be deceived.

Official platforms cut through this illusion. They act as filters, removing many of the most common scams before they ever reach you. While no system is perfect, starting with verified sources shifts the odds dramatically in your favor. Instead of relying on what "looks right," you ground your decisions in what is regulated, monitored, and accountable.

Checking Official Job Boards — Real Work, Real Pay

When searching for employment, it's tempting to apply to every opening you see online. Scammers count on this—placing ads on unverified job boards, social media, or even sending direct emails that appear to come from real companies. The easiest defense is to focus your search on **official job boards** and trusted employment platforms.

Examples include:

- Government-run portals like USAJobs.gov (United States), Job Bank (Canada), or their equivalents worldwide.
- Established, well-known recruitment sites that vet employers before posting.
- Direct company websites—large organizations almost always list their jobs on their own career pages.

Why this matters: verified job boards have strict posting requirements. Employers must go through validation processes, and many fake offers are filtered out. Even when fraud slips through, official platforms provide clear reporting tools so suspicious postings can be removed quickly.

Another important defense: when in doubt, contact the company directly. If you receive an offer out of nowhere, go to the organization's official website (not the link provided in the email) and verify the posting. If it doesn't exist there, it's almost certainly a scam.

Government Sites for Debt Relief — Trusted Lifelines

Debt relief is one of the most emotionally charged areas for scams. The promise of freedom from bills or collectors feels irresistible when you're under pressure. Scammers know this and disguise themselves as trusted authorities. Some even use names that sound like government agencies.

That is why the safest move is to begin with **official government sites** when seeking financial relief. These sites list legitimate programs, accredited credit counseling agencies, and nonprofit resources. In the U.S., for example, the Federal Trade Commission (FTC) and the Consumer Financial Protection Bureau (CFPB) provide clear guidance and warnings about scams. Many countries maintain similar consumer protection agencies with databases of licensed providers.

The difference between a scam and a real program often comes down to two things:

1. **Transparency.** Real programs explain risks, timelines, and limitations. Fraudulent ones promise instant results.
2. **Payment structure.** Licensed organizations may charge fees, but they are regulated, disclosed upfront, and tied to actual services—not demanded immediately before anything begins.

By starting with government resources, you bypass the noise of fraudulent ads and reach providers who have already been vetted.

Combining Skepticism with Structure

Even when using official boards and government sites, maintaining a skeptical mindset is essential. Ask yourself:

- Does the opportunity make sense compared to the industry standard?
- Are the promises realistic, or do they sound too perfect?
- Am I being pressured to act quickly without time for verification?

Legitimate opportunities withstand questioning. Scams fall apart when faced with scrutiny. Remember that trust should be earned, not assumed.

Practical Steps for Everyday Protection

1. **Bookmark official resources.** Save links to your government's employment and debt relief sites so you don't end up on fake lookalikes.
2. **Cross-check job listings.** If you see a posting on a third-party site, verify it directly on the company's official career page.
3. **Look for licensing.** Debt relief providers should display registration numbers or accreditation details, which you can confirm through government databases.
4. **Report suspicious offers.** Most official platforms allow you to flag scams, protecting others from the same trap.
5. **Never pay upfront.** Whether for jobs or debt help, any demand for money before results is a universal red flag.

The Takeaway

Fraudsters thrive in the shadows of uncertainty—on unofficial sites, in private messages, and in ads designed to mimic legitimacy. The simplest and most powerful way to fight back is to step into the light of official sources. By checking job offers against verified boards and turning to government sites for debt relief, you create a buffer between yourself and manipulation.

Growth here means trading desperation for discipline. Instead of rushing toward the first solution that appears, you learn to pause, check, and confirm. Real opportunities don't hide from scrutiny—they invite it. Fake ones collapse when exposed to verification. By rooting your search for work and financial stability in official platforms, you not only protect your money—you protect your hope, ensuring it is invested in real possibilities instead of empty promises.

CHAPTER 8

Identity Theft & Your Defenses

Theft in Plain Sight — Skimming, Fake ATMs, and Phishing Combos

Not all scams arrive in emails or suspicious text messages. Some are carried out in the most ordinary places—at the gas pump, the ATM, or even on websites that look completely legitimate. These scams work because they blend seamlessly into routines we perform without thinking. Among the most common and damaging of these are **skimming**, **fake ATMs**, and **phishing combinations** that merge digital deception with real-world tactics. They target not just money but trust—the assumption that familiar machines and transactions are safe.

Skimming — Data Theft at the Swipe

Skimming occurs when criminals secretly install devices on payment terminals—like gas pumps, ATMs, or even point-of-sale machines at stores. These devices copy card information as soon as it's swiped or inserted. Victims often have no idea anything is wrong until unauthorized charges appear on their statements.

The reason skimming is so effective is its invisibility. The devices are often small, well-camouflaged, and designed to blend with the machine's exterior. In some cases, they're accompanied by tiny cameras or fake keypads that capture PIN numbers.

For example, law enforcement has uncovered skimming devices that fit perfectly over ATM card slots, complete with realistic branding. A casual user might never notice. By the time the fraud is discovered, the card data may already be sold on black markets or used for online purchases.

The red flags are subtle but detectable:

- Card slots that feel loose, bulky, or misaligned.
- Keypads that look raised or hard to press.
- Machines located in isolated or poorly lit areas.

The defense is vigilance: using ATMs in well-monitored locations, tugging gently at card slots before inserting a card, and covering the keypad while entering a PIN.

Fake ATMs — Machines Built for Theft

Some criminals skip modifying existing machines and instead install entirely **fake ATMs.** These can appear in convenience stores, bars, or even on busy sidewalks. At first glance, they look authentic—complete with screens, logos, and card slots. But instead of dispensing cash, they simply collect card data and PINs.

The scam works because most people don't question the existence of an ATM in a familiar setting. The fraudsters rely on convenience: if you're in a hurry and see a machine nearby, you're unlikely to walk to a bank to confirm its legitimacy.

The main warning signs of fake ATMs include:

- Machines placed in unusual or temporary locations.
- ATMs that only accept magnetic swipes (not chip cards).
- Screens with spelling errors, strange messages, or poor graphics.

The best protection is sticking to ATMs at banks or trusted retail chains, which are more secure and regularly inspected.

Phishing Combos — Digital and Physical Deception

Phishing typically refers to fraudulent emails or texts that trick users into clicking malicious links. But modern scammers often combine phishing with real-world tactics, creating hybrid attacks. For example:

- A phishing email might warn, *"Your ATM card has been compromised. Please re-enter your details at this link."* The link leads to a fake banking site that collects login credentials.
- After stealing card data through skimming, scammers may follow up with phishing calls posing as the bank, asking for additional verification codes.
- In some cases, criminals pair fake ATMs with text alerts. After someone uses the machine, they receive a fraudulent "bank notification" pushing them to share security information.

These combos succeed because they layer deception. Each element reinforces the illusion of legitimacy. Victims feel as if they are in constant communication with their bank, unaware that all contact is being orchestrated by criminals.

Why These Schemes Work

Skimming, fake ATMs, and phishing combos succeed because they exploit routine. People expect ATMs to work, card swipes to be safe, and bank alerts to be genuine. By blending into these expectations, scammers avoid suspicion.

The psychological levers include:

- **Trust in infrastructure.** Machines with logos or familiar placements are assumed to be secure.
- **Time pressure.** ATMs and payment machines are often used in hurried moments, when people are less observant.
- **Authority mimicry.** Fake banking messages or ATM interfaces exploit the trust we place in official institutions.

Defenses That Work

1. **Stick to trusted locations.** Use ATMs at banks or busy, well-monitored areas. Avoid isolated or suspiciously placed machines.
2. **Inspect before using.** Tug gently on card slots, check for loose keypads, and look for unusual attachments.
3. **Cover your PIN.** Always shield the keypad with your hand, even if you don't notice a camera.
4. **Monitor accounts.** Set up alerts for every card transaction so you can spot suspicious charges immediately.
5. **Verify bank messages.** If you receive an alert, ignore links and call your bank directly using the official number.

The Takeaway

Skimming devices, fake ATMs, and phishing combos remind us that fraud doesn't only live online—it exists in the spaces we move through every day. These scams are effective because they blend into routine, exploiting trust in familiar actions like withdrawing cash or swiping a card. Growth here means sharpening awareness without succumbing to paranoia. By pausing to inspect, sticking to official channels, and verifying before reacting, you transform everyday vulnerability into everyday resilience.

The ordinary act of paying for gas or using an ATM should not cost your financial security. With vigilance and consistent habits, you ensure that these moments remain safe—and that fraudsters lose their grip on the ordinary.

Red Flags of ATM and Card Scams — When the System Turns Against You

Skimming devices, fake ATMs, and phishing combinations are dangerous not only because of the technology behind them, but because of how invisible they are in everyday life. Unlike scams that rely on bold promises or dramatic threats, these schemes hide in plain sight. The warning signs are subtle, but they're there for anyone who knows how to look. Among the most important red flags are **unexpected charges** and **requests for PINs.** These signals may seem small, but together they expose some of the most damaging financial frauds of the modern era.

Unexpected Charges — The Silent Alarm

Most people first discover they've been targeted by a skimmer or a fake ATM not at the machine itself, but later—when reviewing their bank statement. A meal you never purchased, an online order you didn't place, or a withdrawal in a city you've never visited suddenly appears. These unexpected charges are not just minor annoyances—they're often the first visible proof of theft.

Criminals count on victims ignoring small charges. A few dollars here, ten dollars there. These "test" transactions are used to confirm that the stolen card data is active before larger withdrawals are attempted. If the account holder doesn't notice or report them quickly, scammers escalate.

The psychology here is subtle. Many people glance at their statements without examining every line, especially if the amounts are small. Some even assume they've simply forgotten a purchase. But ignoring these signs gives fraudsters the time they need to drain accounts more aggressively.

The defense is vigilance:

- Set up transaction alerts through your bank's app or SMS system.
- Review your account weekly, line by line.
- Treat even the smallest unexplained charge as suspicious—because it almost always is.

Unexpected charges aren't random mistakes. They are breadcrumbs left behind by someone exploiting your financial trust.

Requests for PINs — The Illusion of Legitimacy

The second universal red flag is any request for your PIN (Personal Identification Number) outside of the secure ATM or point-of-sale transaction. Scammers use both technology and social engineering to trick people into surrendering this critical piece of information.

In skimming scams, hidden cameras or fake keypads are installed to capture PINs as they are entered. In phishing schemes, fraudsters pose as banks, sending emails or texts that say: *"For security purposes, please verify your PIN."* Some even call victims directly, claiming to be from fraud prevention teams and asking for verification.

The danger lies in how natural these requests can sound. Because they appear to come from trusted institutions, people let down their guard. But here's the unshakable truth: **no legitimate bank or financial institution will ever ask for your PIN outside of a secure, encrypted transaction.** If someone is requesting it—whether through a message, a call, or an unusual ATM prompt—they are not protecting you. They are stealing from you.

Why These Red Flags Work Together

Unexpected charges and requests for PINs often appear in tandem. A fraudster may first capture card data through a skimmer, then follow up with a phishing call to extract the PIN needed for larger withdrawals. Or, after installing a fake ATM, they may message victims pretending to be "customer service" to "verify unusual activity."

This layered approach is powerful because it creates a false sense of continuity. Victims believe their bank is aware of the fraud and working to stop it—when in reality, the same scammers are orchestrating every step. Each red flag reinforces the other, trapping people in a carefully staged illusion.

How to Respond to These Signals

The most important step is recognizing that these red flags are not isolated inconveniences—they are alarms demanding immediate action. Here's how to respond:

1. **If you see unexpected charges, act fast.** Contact your bank immediately, freeze your card, and request a replacement. The sooner you respond, the less damage is done.
2. **Never share your PIN.** Not over the phone, not in an email, not through a text link. If asked, end the interaction immediately.

3. **Change passwords and PINs regularly.** Even if you haven't been targeted, rotating credentials reduces long-term risk.
4. **Report phishing attempts.** Forward suspicious messages to your bank's fraud department or national reporting services.
5. **Trust behavior, not appearance.** A message, machine, or call may look official, but the request itself reveals the truth. If it asks for a PIN outside of normal use, it's fraudulent.

The Takeaway

Theft through skimming, fake ATMs, and phishing is sophisticated in design but simple in execution. Scammers don't need you to make big mistakes—just to ignore small red flags. Unexpected charges and requests for PINs are those signals. They may appear subtle, but they represent the dividing line between safety and exploitation.

Growth here means developing habits of observation. It's about turning routine actions—checking statements, using ATMs, responding to messages—into opportunities for vigilance. By treating every unexplained charge as suspicious and refusing to share PINs under any circumstance, you build a protective barrier that scammers cannot easily penetrate.

Fraudsters thrive on silence and compliance. The moment you notice, question, and act, you break their cycle. What feels like a minor inconvenience—double-checking your statement or saying no to a suspicious request—becomes an act of empowerment. And in that small act, you not only protect your money—you protect your trust in yourself to navigate a world where deception often hides in plain sight.

Building Strong Financial Defenses — Monitoring, 2FA, and Credit Freezes

Scammers evolve constantly, finding new ways to exploit technology, payment systems, and even our daily routines. From skimming devices at ATMs to phishing combos that merge emails with fake calls, their strategies rely on slipping past attention and exploiting moments of vulnerability. But the truth is this: while no system is completely immune, individuals have more defensive power than they often realize. Three of the most effective tools available today are **monitoring financial accounts regularly, enabling two-factor authentication (2FA), and using credit freezes when necessary.** Together, these form a layered defense that protects not just money in the present but also long-term identity security.

Monitor Accounts — Catch the Small Before It Becomes Big

Most scams don't start with massive withdrawals. Criminals often test stolen card data with small purchases—$1, $3, $10—just to confirm the account is active. If those charges go unnoticed, they escalate to larger amounts or sell the card details on black markets. For this reason, consistent monitoring is one of the most powerful defenses.

Practical steps include:

- **Daily or weekly checks.** Take five minutes to scan recent transactions through your bank's app or online portal. Treat it as part of your routine.
- **Enable alerts.** Most banks offer text or app notifications for every charge, regardless of amount. This real-time feedback ensures you spot fraud within minutes instead of weeks.
- **Don't ignore the small stuff.** A $2 charge from a vendor you don't recognize is not harmless—it's a test run. By reporting it immediately, you stop larger theft before it happens.

The psychological advantage of monitoring is equally important. Instead of feeling blindsided by fraud, you stay in control, turning financial vigilance into empowerment rather than fear.

Two-Factor Authentication (2FA) — Adding a Gate

Passwords alone are no longer enough. Data breaches, phishing emails, and credential leaks happen daily, putting usernames and passwords at constant risk. Two-factor authentication (2FA) adds a critical extra step—something you have in addition to something you know.

Forms of 2FA include:

- **Text message codes** sent to your phone.
- **Authentication apps** like Google Authenticator, Authy, or Microsoft Authenticator, which generate time-sensitive codes.
- **Biometric checks,** such as fingerprint or facial recognition on mobile devices.

Even if scammers obtain your password, they cannot log in without the second factor. This drastically reduces the success rate of phishing attempts and credential stuffing attacks. For maximum protection, use app-based or hardware token authentication, as text messages can sometimes be intercepted through SIM-swapping scams.

The principle is simple: make the lock harder to pick. A password alone is a basic key. Adding 2FA is like installing a deadbolt.

Credit Freeze — The Nuclear Option When Necessary

Sometimes fraud goes beyond unauthorized charges—it targets your identity. Criminals with enough personal information can open new credit cards, take out loans, or even rent property in your name. These forms of fraud can devastate credit scores and take years to repair.

A **credit freeze** is one of the most powerful tools available to prevent this. When your credit is frozen, no lender can open new accounts under your identity without your direct approval. Even if scammers possess your Social Security number, birth date, and address, they hit a wall when trying to extend credit.

Important details:

- **It's free.** In most countries, credit bureaus allow you to place or lift freezes at no cost.
- **It doesn't affect existing accounts.** Your current cards and loans remain usable.
- **You control the timing.** If you need to apply for credit, you can temporarily lift the freeze for a specific period.

A freeze isn't always necessary, but it's wise in high-risk situations: if your personal data was leaked in a breach, if your wallet was stolen, or if you've already experienced identity theft. Think of it as the strongest barrier available when other defenses have been compromised.

Why These Defenses Work Best Together

Each tool—monitoring, 2FA, and credit freezes—addresses a different layer of risk. Monitoring catches fraud quickly, 2FA prevents unauthorized logins, and credit freezes block identity theft before it escalates. Separately, each adds value. Combined, they form a system that makes you a far harder target.

Scammers thrive on easy victims. They rely on people who don't check their statements, who reuse weak passwords without 2FA, and who leave their credit wide open even after data breaches. By adopting these three practices, you shift yourself out of that vulnerable category. Fraudsters, faced with resistance, are more likely to move on to easier prey.

The Takeaway

Financial security in the digital age doesn't come from trusting systems blindly—it comes from active participation. By monitoring accounts regularly, enabling two-factor authentication, and using credit freezes when needed, you create a layered shield against theft. These habits are not complicated, but they are powerful.

Growth here means moving from a passive relationship with your finances to an active one. Instead of reacting to fraud after it happens, you take steps that anticipate and block it. This shift transforms financial vulnerability into confidence. You're no longer hoping that your bank or credit company protects you—you're joining them as your own first line of defense.

Scams are inevitable. Fraud attempts will continue. But their success is not guaranteed. With awareness and consistent action, you make their job infinitely harder. And in doing so, you protect not only your money but also the peace of mind that comes from knowing you are in control.

CONCLUSION

The Red Flag Rulebook

The Universal Scam Checklist — Three Signals That Expose Deception

Scams take many forms. Some arrive as emails claiming to be from your bank. Others appear as phone calls, fake job postings, or even glossy investment pitches. Technology changes, trends evolve, but the mechanics of fraud remain surprisingly consistent. Beneath the details, almost every scam relies on the same three levers: **urgency, secrecy, and money requests.** These are the fingerprints of manipulation, showing up again and again regardless of context. By learning to recognize them, you gain a powerful tool—a universal checklist that can expose deception before it costs you.

Urgency — The Pressure to Act Now

The first and most common red flag is urgency. Scammers know that thinking is the enemy of manipulation. If you stop to reflect, check details, or consult others, their illusion collapses. That's why they push speed above all else.

You'll hear phrases like:

- *"Act now or lose everything."*
- *"This opportunity expires tonight."*
- *"If you don't respond immediately, your account will be suspended."*

The tactic is psychological. Urgency activates the brain's survival instincts, shifting decision-making from the rational prefrontal cortex to the reactive amygdala. Under time pressure, people are more likely to make impulsive choices. Research confirms that humans consistently favor immediate action when under deadlines, even when waiting would produce better outcomes.

This explains why urgency is used everywhere—from phishing emails demanding instant login verification to door-to-door scams insisting a roof repair must be paid for "today only." The details change, but the mechanism is the same. If someone is forcing you to decide without time to verify, that pressure is a red flag.

Secrecy — "Don't Tell Anyone"

The second universal tactic is secrecy. Fraudsters often frame their pitch as privileged information or insist that victims keep the interaction private. This may sound like:

- *"This is confidential—don't share with anyone else."*
- *"You've been specially selected for this opportunity."*
- *"If you tell your bank or family, they'll just confuse you or block the process."*

Secrecy works because it isolates victims. By cutting them off from outside input, scammers prevent reality checks. Friends, family, or colleagues could easily point out inconsistencies, but the victim is pressured to keep things hidden.

This pattern appears in romance scams, where the fraudster demands loyalty through secrecy. It shows up in Ponzi schemes, where participants are told the investment is "exclusive." And it is present in phishing, where victims are instructed not to question the communication but to act through the provided link only.

Healthy opportunities do not fear transparency. Real businesses and institutions welcome questions, encourage consultation, and provide documentation. If secrecy is part of the pitch, deception almost certainly is too.

Money Requests — The Final Step

The third and most critical red flag is a request for money. It might be immediate, like a demand for gift cards or wire transfers, or more subtle, like fees for training, taxes, or processing. No matter the disguise, the pattern is always the same: the scam leads inexorably to payment.

These requests often come after urgency and secrecy have already done their work. Once victims feel rushed and isolated, they are more likely to surrender money. The psychology here draws on the *consistency principle*: if you've already invested time, energy, or emotional commitment, you're more likely to justify giving money to stay aligned with your previous choices.

But the truth is simple: legitimate opportunities do not hinge on upfront payments or hidden fees. Jobs pay you, not the other way around. Banks and governments never demand gift cards. Real investments explain risks openly instead of guaranteeing profits. If a situation ends with *"send money now,"* you're not looking at opportunity—you're looking at exploitation.

Using the Checklist in Daily Life

The beauty of this three-part checklist is its universality. Whether you're facing a phone call from a supposed tax agent, a flashy crypto investment, or a stranger sliding into your messages, the same questions apply:

1. **Am I being rushed to act?**
2. **Am I being told to keep this secret?**
3. **Am I being asked for money?**

If the answer to even one is "yes," pause. If the answer to two or three is "yes," assume a scam until proven otherwise.

This doesn't mean you should live in paranoia. Many legitimate situations involve deadlines, privacy, or payments. The difference is context and transparency. A real university may require tuition, but it provides contracts, accreditation, and time for consideration. A real employer may expect confidentiality, but not to the point of isolating you from your support network. A real business may run limited promotions, but they won't collapse under basic questions or independent verification.

The Takeaway

Fraud thrives on complexity, but its core tactics are simple. Urgency, secrecy, and money requests are the three threads woven into almost every scam. By training yourself to look for these signals, you create a filter that cuts through surface details and exposes manipulation at its core.

Growth here means learning to pause where scammers demand speed, to share where they demand secrecy, and to withhold money where they demand payment without proof. This universal checklist is not just about avoiding loss—it's about strengthening your ability to navigate a world full of noise, pressure, and false promises with calm clarity.

With urgency resisted, secrecy broken, and money protected, scams lose their leverage. What remains is your ability to choose deliberately, to protect what matters, and to invest your trust only where it truly belongs.

Reassurance in the Fight Against Scams — Evolving Tricks, Unchanging Patterns

At first glance, scams can feel overwhelming. Every week, news headlines highlight new frauds: crypto collapses, AI-powered phishing, fake investment apps, or cloned voices used in phone scams. The sheer variety creates the impression that criminals are always one step ahead, adapting faster than the rest of us can learn. But here's the reassuring truth: while scams evolve in surface detail, their underlying patterns remain the same. Once you recognize those patterns, you gain a lasting defense that applies across generations, technologies, and trends.

The Illusion of Innovation

Scammers are skilled at making their tricks look new. In the 1920s, Charles Ponzi promised profits through international postage stamps. A century later, others promise wealth through digital tokens, NFTs, or AI projects. On the surface, the packaging looks different—old-world paper schemes versus futuristic algorithms. But underneath, the structure is identical: early participants are paid with the funds of later ones until the system collapses.

This is the illusion of innovation. Fraudsters wrap timeless manipulations in the language of whatever era they're in. Where once they mailed letters, now they send emails. Where once they posed as tax agents at the door, now they spoof phone numbers. What changes is the tool. What stays the same is the psychology: urgency, secrecy, and requests for money.

Why Patterns Persist

Why don't scammers truly innovate? Because human psychology doesn't change. Whether in 1924 or 2024, people respond predictably to the same triggers:

- **Fear of loss.** "Act now or lose everything."
- **Hope of gain.** "Invest now and get rich."
- **Trust in authority.** "This is your bank. Follow instructions."
- **Need for belonging.** "Don't tell anyone—this is just for you."

These levers work across cultures, generations, and technologies. As long as human beings carry the same emotional wiring, scams don't need to evolve their essence—only their disguise.

The Power of Pattern Recognition

This is where reassurance lies. You don't need to memorize every new fraud that emerges. Instead, you need to train your mind to notice the recurring signals: urgency, secrecy, and financial requests. These are the fingerprints left on nearly every scam, regardless of the story being told.

Think of it like learning to read music. The notes may be arranged in endless combinations, but once you understand the scale, you can interpret any song. Scams are the same: once you see the underlying pattern, the surface details no longer confuse you.

Resilience in Practice

To turn this reassurance into daily protection, a few habits make the difference:

1. **Pause when pressured.** If urgency is the main tactic, slowing down is the counter-move.

2. **Break secrecy.** Share suspicious messages with friends, family, or colleagues. Scams collapse when exposed to a second set of eyes.
3. **Guard your money.** Refuse any payment requests that bypass official, verifiable systems.

These habits are timeless. They worked against door-to-door cons in the 19th century, against email scams in the 2000s, and they will work against AI-enabled frauds tomorrow.

The Takeaway

Yes, scams evolve. The tools get sharper, the stories get slicker, and the disguises get harder to spot. But beneath the surface, the playbook barely changes. Urgency, secrecy, and money requests remain the pillars of manipulation. That truth should not frighten you—it should reassure you. Because once you know the patterns, you can recognize them no matter how they're dressed up.

Growth in this area means shifting from fear to confidence. Instead of worrying about every new fraud making headlines, you remind yourself that the rules haven't changed. Scammers can update their costumes, but their script is the same. And once you've learned to read that script, you carry a defense that lasts a lifetime.

Thank You

Thank you for taking the time to read this book. I wrote it with one goal in mind: to give you tools that protect your money, your time, and your peace of mind. If these pages helped you see scams more clearly, recognize red flags faster, or feel more confident in your ability to protect yourself, then this book has done its job.

Your feedback matters more than you might realize. Reviews not only help other readers decide whether this book is worth their time, they also help spread the message that we *can* outsmart scams and grow stronger through awareness.

If you found value here, I would be deeply grateful if you could take a few minutes to leave an honest review. Share what you learned, which parts stood out, or how it helped you in your own life. Every review makes a difference.

Thank you again for trusting me to be part of your journey toward growth and resilience. Stay aware, stay confident, and keep growing.

Eric LeBouthillier